ABOUT THE AUTHOR

Genevieve Carver is a Sheffield-based poet searching for the humanity amidst the chaos. Her work has appeared in publications including *Iota*, *Envoi*, and *The North*. Genevieve Carver & The Unsung are a multi-disciplinary performance project celebrating unsung heroes and marginal voices. They are double winners of Buxton Fringe Spoken Word Award and released their first studio album in 2017.

Website: https://www.genevievecarver.com/
Twitter: @Gevicarver

Genevieve Carver
A Beautiful Way to be Crazy
and other poems from the stage

VERVE
POETRY PRESS
BIRMINGHAM

PUBLISHED BY VERVE POETRY PRESS
https://vervepoetrypress.com
mail@vervepoetrypress.com

All rights reserved
© 2020 Genevieve Carver

The right of Genevieve Carver to be identified as author of this work has been asserted in accordance with section 77 of the Copyright, Designs and Patents Act 1988.

No part of this work may be reproduced, stored or transmitted in any form or by any means, graphic, electronic, recorded or mechanical, without the prior written permission of the publisher.

FIRST PUBLISHED FEB 2020

Printed and bound in the UK
by TJ International, Padstow

ISBN: 978-1-912565-35-1

Cover photo credit: Alexandra Wallace.

To Sheffield

CONTENTS

Recipe for a New Poem	10
Her Heart	12
Waltzes	13
The Writing on the Wall	14
The Office Party	15
Keep On Kicking Against the Pricks	18
Katrina Has a Cleaner Now	20
Why I Don't Do Yoga	23
You Asked Me for a Poem	26
International Heartbreak	28
Turbulence	30
Backpacker	31
People Don't Get Lost Anymore	33
Thank You for Driving Carefully Through Hope	37
Crossed Wires I: Vehicle Insurance	38
Crossed Wires II: Council Tax	41
Thunder and Sunshine	43
If You Know What I Mean	45

From *The Unsung*

Air on a Heartstring	48
The Eagles of Death	50
The Fiery Angel	55
The Unsung	58
Exit Music	61

A Beautiful Way to be Crazy

Prelude	66
It's Alright, Dad (I'm Only Disappearing)	69
This Stage Ain't Big Enough for the Both of Us	72
Human Being (a pop song)	75
Little Green	78
We Don't Need Another Hero	81
Canary in the Coal Mine	84
A Beautiful Way to be Crazy	87
Champagne, Cocaine & Sausages	89

Acknowledgements

A Beautiful Way to be Crazy
and other poems from the stage

Recipe for a New Poem

250g natural imagery
250g inner turmoil
100g assonance
50cl dry London gin

Take one kernel of lucidity, born in the night.

Cush lightly, using your own backbone for a pestle.

Toast together with your thoughts on love
until they blacken, begin to smell like
your grandmother's laundry room.

Add half a pint of longing
and leave to simmer –
the longing should permeate the mixture
until it separates, forming a fine
listless film on the surface.

Remove from the heat and allow to cool.

While waiting, drink the gin.

Make sure to always taste your poem –
if you can't stomach it
how on earth will they.

Once the poem has set
transfer into a relic from your past –
your first skateboard or the diary
with *KEEP OUT* on the cover.

Take it somewhere scenic
rest it on a shingle shore
and allow it to draw in the ocean's breath.

Return home
turn your poem upside-down
and slice it lengthways.

Listen closely for the hiss of misperception.

Serve cold, with lashings of pretext
and slip silently from the kitchen via a side door.

Her Heart

She wears it on her sleeveless dress,
    that one

holds it in the palm of her
        please never let go.

Too busy spilling herself,
she trusts it to dance-floor corners
surfing supermarket trolleys home   alone
        with friends

and falling deep in wanderlust with
everyone she meets
she offers it on a silver *does it matter*
    lets the vultures feed.

Look at her, poor thing;
    they will string her up by her guts.

Waltzes

I wanted to tell you about how I like
waltzes. But something interrupted
us like a bleating phone or *late for work* and

I never finished what I was saying.
It's really nothing
just that it must have been nice

to stop all that prancing about
and look someone in the eyes
for three whole minutes

and gently sway
as I say
doesn't matter anyway.

One
     two
          three.

The Writing on the Wall

Do you remember when we wrote
FUCK YOU HURFORD AND CO. LETTINGS MANAGEMENT
in massive letters on the bedroom wall
before we painted over it
and just before we left the flat
Charlotte said you could still see it
and we said we never gave a shit because we never.

Do you remember when we moved to Solly Street
and had to get rid of the *Emerald Wave*
in the bathroom and you wrote
I LOVE YOU in great big matt emulsion strokes
and I laughed because you wrote it right over the shitter
and you said *that's what you get
for moving to Silly Street.*

Last year I did up the living room
(it's a nice place I have now but my God did it need it)
and I was tempted to write
WHERE ARE YOU NOW
in *Desert Obsession* above the skirting board.
But it felt a bit silly, you know
doing it on my own.

The Office Party

Cheap wine is sipped, tight-lipped
manicured nails, red-tipped
drum hypnotically
on the tall, slender glass
    of tall, slender Glenda the receptionist
conversations tame and clipped
we stick to the script.

Al from Marketing shuffles uncomfortably
stares blankly into moon-face of
long-time colleague and desk-partner Martin

wonders how it is possible
that in all these years
of headaches and deadlines
and dead aches and headlines
and spreadsheets and dead beats
and tea breaks and free cakes
and shared space and scared haste

he has known nothing more of him
than his tailored trousers
    his lemon-meringue ties
        his sugared coffee
           his wife's name.

                                      ...

More wine swallowed
words follow
talk is small at first
though later on
might just be pillow
especially if you believe what they're saying
about Derrick and the intern.

But Katy, the brunette from upstairs
who is on her fifth glass
    her fifteenth Pringle
        her third conversation
about the new canteen
can take it no more.

She begins to talk
and soon she cannot stop

her hopes and dreams   secret talents
lost loves   changed opinions   shameful passions
treasured memories   pet hates

are skittling from her smudged lips
never belied by her true, wide, blue-shadowed eyes.

And she is no longer alone
for Derrick has a saxophone in his bedroom
Al dreams of Mexico on a motorbike
Martin's wife has never found his dressing-up box
or his Lloyd-Weber collection

and tall, slender Glenda – even she
has wondered at one time or another
if there might not be something more

and suddenly they all want to take flight
and all have secret books they'll never write.

Keep on Kicking Against the Pricks

I wasn't there in '68
when Paris shook herself awake
and the streets were filled with pepper spray
and tear-gas and fury and chaos and flames
and the people in the streets were filled with faith
and the hearts in the people in the streets were free.

I wasn't there in Tahrir Square
in the struggle and the smoke and the strife and the stress
in the murder and mess in the sorrow and strain
in the turn of the screw in the twist of the spring
in the *snap* of a camera-phone photograph
of a battered body in a Libyan drain.

I never set myself on fire
and I never fired myself with rage
I never raged against the machine
and I never waged war on the regime
and I never had a dream and I never vented spleen
and I never went on strike and I never fought the fight.

Because I work in middle management
and I manage muddled middle men
and I keep my middle finger down
and I bite my tongue and I nod my head
and I talk on the phone on the train on my break
and I break on the go on my way on my own
and I own a little diary and I pencil people in
and I never forget which day it is.

But nevertheless I've managed to find
the tiniest ways to speak my mind
I'll park my car on a double yellow line
and I'll smoke a cheeky cigarette and tell a little lie
and I'll sing along with Dylan in my headphones on the tube
and I'll call in sick just to stay in bed with you.

And though I didn't always care
and I never did and I wasn't there
I was there last Thursday on my bike
in the pouring rain at the traffic lights
and I saw that they were locked on red
but I just sailed right on ahead.

And I was there in the superstore
in the scramble and scrum and the squeeze and the squash
in the crush and the rush of the Saturday brawl
in the screech of the child and the tired mother's drawl
and I thought to myself as I looked in their eyes
and singled out the single worst offender of them all
there's a firing line in the back of my mind
and you'll be first against the wall.

Katrina Has a Cleaner Now

We meet for coffee
because it symbolises that we're earning now.

We used to make our own
save the pennies for necessities like alcohol
but now we meet for coffee

and a *catch up*
though staring at the drinks board I can already see
that I've got more catching up to do than you

looking so at home with your *mochaccino* foam
on your lipglossed top lip
    dripping gossip sprinkles
        on your sentences like cocoa

whilst I, watching hyperbolic monikers frolicking
quickly calculate that if I get an *espresso macchiato*
I can pretend it's because I want you to see that I know what it is
and not because it's cheap.

I think of when we went round, you and I
scraping off pennies stuck with chuddy
to the bottoms of desks, wondering

when it was we stopped talking
about what we can and can't afford

where the midpoint was between
it becoming no longer ok to bring only two fags
already half smoked by your mother to the party
and this ludicrous display of half your week's wages
casually siphoned off into a *cinnamon Grande latte.*

We sit   and slurp   and sink
as into a tepid bath into our past
summoning up the ghostly shapes
that once inhabited our days

- Lottie's well, she's got an allotment
and the prize shallots to prove it
Caz and Bill have bought a house
Helen's marrying a Tony -

and as your words froth up like steamy milk
I try to guess by peering in between your teeth
and underneath your fingernails
if you still smoke or not

'cause Vicky's quit and so has Chris
Nick's been turkey cold since Christmas
Rickie's seen a hypnotist
but he always was a dreamer

and Knobby's chopped his deadlocks off
and Mo's stone cold more often than not
and Tina's saving for a yacht
and Katrina *has a cleaner now.*

...

I try to focus my attention on your lips
sync their motion to the sounds emitting from them
but somehow my brain, though well primed with caffeine
struggles to make sense of a single word

and my ears, though pricked as pins
can only hear a faint murmur
swimming through the throng
asking *how long can we go on living*
in these ill-fitting skins
how long before we spin
   out of orbit

now Katrina has a cleaner
does that change the game for good
are we no longer after the absolute
are we stopping short of the real and the raw
what happened to the point of no return
and what about the blue sky
   and the revolution?

And I know that two won't fit on a ladder
but doesn't it make you smile to think
of how we once would've tried
   four feet on a rung and happy to risk it
      all too critically airborne.

And I know the midnight shopping trolley express
lies rusted and forgotten now
in the bed of a small-town canal
but throw me a rope
and I'd still surf it drunkenly home
if I thought that you'd come with me.

Why I Don't Do Yoga

Because sometimes a bottle of South African red
and a 20-deck of B & H Gold
does more to keep the stitching from unravelling.

Because some mornings are made
for crying on public transport
parking fines   missed alarms
locking your keys inside   locking yourself outside
finding thee-day old vomit on your jacket
finding three-day old vomit in your hair
finding yourself unable to explain the presence
     of two broken swivel chairs
          of one swivelled stranger in your living room
finding yourself bruised and unwashed
not finding yourself.

Because you can't salute the sun
when the sky is dank as Manchester
and the ground beneath your feet keeps shifting
and your hands repel each other   like two negative magnets.

Because I've had more last ever cigarettes
than first days of diets
because when the waves come crashing in
sinking makes way more sense than swimming.

...

Because it's Sunday afternoon
and I haven't been to bed
went out for one on Friday
now every time I move my head
the whole thing rattles
as if actual screws are loose in there

there's a hazy bit somewhere around Saturday
but I'm pretty sure it was after trying to set fire to Charlie
that I got into a real funk
I tried to shag the barman
but he said I was too drunk
now everything I'm wearing is covered in shite
and I've lost another earring down the back of the night.

Because I will never be one of those quiet, sensible humans
that seem to watch me from the cracks between calamities
the ones that occupy the sofa seats in cafés
with laptops   haircuts   flat whites
disposable income   five-year plans
the ones not saying stupid things
or messing up each others' lives.

Because sometimes weak and wobbly will just have to do
fuck *Strong and Stable*.

Because it's Tuesday morning
and I still haven't been to bed.

Because I can't remember who I am
which bits of me are real
because I want to run a million miles
and dive into the sea
because it reminds me of P.E.
because it makes me feel inadequate
because of some painful thing I can't remember
that happened when I was small
because   it   hurts.

Because I want to stand, perilous and bare
like a lonely house on a heather-clad moor
feel the wind roar through my dry stone walls
to the tune of *still not good enough, Carver.*

Because I've got half a brain
because I'm into champagne
because deep breaths   on their own
                              are hard enough.

You Asked Me for a Poem

and I was going to give you
the one I wake up gasping every winter
where I splurt my soul out onto the briny sheets
crying though the mucus and the flood of fears
that *I am sorry*
I hadn't known the element was hot
I never meant to scald him.

I was going read the one I saw
etched on the bones of someone that I used to love
when I crawled inside his ribcage for the last time

or the one they taught me when I visited Europa
as we sipped on cocktails made from mercury
and laughed among the stars

or the one where all the sadness in the world
is trampled into the rotting leaves
and sunlight is allowed to creep in through the trees again.

I wanted to tell you everything
hand it all over
say *you   you deal with this*
take it   make something better
than I know how
take it   make it better
make it matter   make it stop.

I sailed a thousand miles to get to you
through raging storms of
talkingallnightlong   dancingtothewrongmusic
dancingwiththewronglimbs   wrongpeople
reeling   sliding   falling   writhing
getting up   falling   laughing   crying
falling

and somewhere along the way
I was thrown like spray from the deck
but even the ocean was not big enough to drown in
so from there I walked, knee-deep in bleak liquid
and calling out your name like a ghost in the shallows

just to give you the poem I can't
the poem that won't come

so I just said
I'm not in the mood for poems right now
fixed my eyes   back   on the floor.

International Heartbreak

We
were
separated by
a thin strip
of black nylon   s t r e t c h e d   between metal posts
distinguishing the end of the Departures Lounge
from the beginning of Security Procedures.

Those not intending to travel may not pass this point.

My lips
were
pulled from yours by
the cruel words of
some stone-hearted stone-headed
sun-glassed sun-hatted sun-seeker.

Are you in the queue?

Yes
I was
and it was moving out of reach
and as your hand released mine I felt hot tears
and I thought they must be toxic because they burned my face
so I bottled them up in 100ml containers
and made sure to seal them in a clear plastic bag
and as I went through the machine of course it beeped

and I could still see you standing there
as I took off my belt and thought about how you'd taken it off
the night before and how you'd run your hands down my body
as the slim-boned Easy-Jet *easy-does-it* attendant was doing now
only her hands were rough and cold.

I could still see you
as, having identified the problem
she calmly removed my heart
and passed it through the X-ray scanner
in a tray with my keys, wallet and mobile phone.

I could still see you
as I turned the corner towards Gate 47
where a *safety-first first-in-line*
not-like-that not-in-my-country airport official
was to formally inform me that
I could not take my soul on the plane
and then

I couldn't see you anymore.

Turbulence

Imagine if I DIEd
and you were the last one
not to have   given a flying   fUCK
     got to shrrrrug your memory
sO As not to stain my death with it
never mind clean knickers   if we're aiming
   for   NirVANa   we'll have to wipe the time
in your Skoda Fabia   and the   time
I W AITed for you to grow up
     for a   t h o u s a ndYEARS
if I hit the deck so hard my brains came o u t
     of my   aRSe
         would you give a damn then,
           Wo U L d   y O U ? ¿

Backpacker

Knows his way round a temple
gets local rates because he's learnt the lingo
doesn't flinch at grasshoppers for breakfast.

Treks tracks off the beaten
backbone aches, coca makes
his head level.

Hash in a chillum like in Sikkim
where they believe tobacco
is the pubic hair of demons.

Full moon, spring tide
having the time of his
                lies
                              awake at night sometimes

alive in dreamtime, softly treads a songline
while his guitar gently
doesn't miss him mum at all.

Twinkle in his *I've seen a thing or two*
hand was always up at school
teacher knew he'd *go somewhere.*

                                                      ...

Wisdom got from scrawny man
on mountain top
won't tell you what it is

though for all he knows
Yogi's on his third divorce
and only up there to evade the child care bill.

People Don't Get Lost Anymore

At the roundabout, take the third exit.

In 400 yards, turn left.
Here you will find a confusing one-way system
with poorly signposted onward routes.

Go round it twice, at least.

Turn to your passenger
ask him to help you get the hell out of there.

Ask him again, with more urgency this time –
the driver is allowed to raise her voice.

At the roundabout, take the fourth exit.
Find yourself on an unlikely back road
littered with potholes and broken glass.
Try not to think of all the things that terrified you as a child.

Where possible, make a U-turn.
Where possible, try to unsay all the things you wish you'd never said.
Where possible, take your foot out of your mouth –
put it back on the clutch before anyone sees.

In 400 yards, take a left you're pretty sure you've already tried.
Swear under your breath, then out loud.

Update your Facebook status to *LOST*.

At the roundabout, try not to forget who you are and where you came from.
Keep going round until you can remember, or it makes you sick.
At the roundabout, try not to forget where you're going.
Keep going round. Your destination is unavailable.
Keep going round. Your destination is –
where possible, make a U-turn.

Ask your passenger to *use the fucking map*.
Veer wildly onto the wrong side of the carriageway
and narrowly miss the oncoming traffic.
Tell your passenger he's *as much use as a useless piece of useless fucking shit*.
Open the passenger door and throw him into the road.

Update your Facebook status to *LOST AND ALONE*.

Rev the engine aggressively
and screech off towards the horizon.
Feel the heat of the day slide away
watch the sky fall through the sunroof
the moon slicing upwards through the darkthick dark.
Turn on your headlights.

Update your Facebook status to *LOST AND ALONE AT NIGHT*.

Where possible, make a U-turn.
Go back in search of your passenger.
Try to let him know that you are sorry
you've made a terrible mistake
but you can make it up to him.

Write him a letter
tell him you wish it hadn't had to end this way
and seal it with a kiss.

Tear the letter into a thousand pieces
and throw them out of the window.

In 400 yards, have a crisis of identity.
Grow a beard   join a band   get fit   get hip
change your name   change your perfume
change your knickers   change your life.
Get a tattoo   get pregnant   get divorced
get loaded   have a good time
be free   be whoever you want to be.

Quit your job   quit smoking
quit drinking so much you wake up
without any shoes or any friends
quit waking up in a kebab
quit waking up with a stranger
learn to wake up with yourself
learn to love waking up with yourself
learn to love yourself.

Update your Facebook status to
LOST AND ALONE AT NIGHT AND FEELING LOVED

At the roundabout, take the third exit.
Your destination is on the right.

The clouds are blushing pink and one by one the stars bow out.
To your right you see a picnic table
some Subway wrappers rustling in the morning breeze.
The park gates are shut
across them hangs a red-lettered sign
in language you don't recognize.

Something, perhaps a fox, is snuffling
in the bushes near the overflowing bin.

Turn the key in the ignition.
In 400 yards, turn left.

Thank You for Driving Carefully Through Hope

Jarvis Cocker is going on about sex and disappointment
whispering *Hackenthorpe* through the disappointing
plastic car speakers as if he were breathing French perfume
down my neck. You told me I couldn't go on living life
as if I were a Jarvis Cocker lyric but the first time
we slept together you hit me – you didn't ask
because you knew I wanted it so in a way
weren't you contributing to the problem?
The shock absorbers are drinking in the road
and it turns out being let down wasn't just a '90s thing.
Unfortunately we couldn't find space for you in this issue.
...so please can I ask just why we're alive
cos all that you do seems such a waste of time
and if you hang around too long...

Crossed Wires I: Vehicle Insurance

WHAT IS YOUR FULL NAME AND ADDRESS
WHAT GENDER ARE YOU
WHAT SEXUALITY
ARE YOU SURE

WHAT STAR SIGN
WHICH CHINESE YEAR

ARE YOU MARRIED
WELL THEN HAVE YOU HAD A BOYFRIEND RECENTLY
DO YOU KNOW YOUR WAY AROUND A WASHING MACHINE
CAN YOU PAIR UP SOCKS AND CHANGE A NAPPY AT THE
    SAME TIME

ARE YOU A HOMEOWNER
WOULD YOU DESCRIBE YOUR INTERIOR FURNISHINGS AS
    RANDOMLY SELECTED   OR
    BELONGING TO A DELIBERATE COLOUR SCHEME
DO YOU EVER GO INTO THE LOUNGE WITH YOUR
    SHOES ON

HAVE YOU BEEN A UK RESIDENT SINCE BIRTH
HAVE YOU EVER HARBOURED DISLOYAL FEELINGS ABOUT
    BRITISH SOIL
    LIKE WISHING YOU'D BEEN BORN SOMEWHERE
        WARMER   OR
    ASPIRING TO LEARN ANOTHER LANGUAGE

HAVE YOU MADE ANY CLAIMS REGARDLESS OF BLAME   OR
   HAD ANY MOTORING CONVICTIONS IN THE LAST
      FIVE YEARS
HAVE YOU EVER FARTED AND BLAMED SOMEONE ELSE

HAVE YOU EVER GONE TO BED WITHOUT BRUSHING
   YOUR TEETH
HAVE YOU EVER PHONED IN SICK
HAVE YOU EVER DRUNK A WHOLE BOTTLE OF RED WINE
   ON YOUR OWN
HOW MANY TIMES

HAVE YOU EVER SMOKED A CIGARETTE MADE OUT OF THE
   STUB ENDS OF OTHER CIGARETTES
WERE ALL THE STUBBIES AT LEAST YOUR OWN

IF YOU WERE A DESSERT, WOULD YOU BE
   A) A TIRAMISU
   B) A TREACLE SPONGE
   C) HALF A JAR OF PEANUT BUTTER, EATEN WITH
      A SPOON   OR
   D) A TIN OF READY-MADE RICE PUDDING, COLD, EATEN
      WITH YOUR BARE HANDS

WHICH WAS YOUR FAVOURITE TELLY-TUBBY

WHICH PASTIME DO YOU PREFER
   A) WATCHING SEX IN THE CITY
   B) ZUMBA   OR
   C) STABBING YOURSELF REPEATEDLY IN THE LEG WITH
A BLUNT STANLEY KNIFE

                                                                   ...

WOULD YOU RATHER BE STRANDED ON A DESERT
    ISLAND WITH
    A) ANDY MURRAY
    B) NIGELLA LAWSON   OR
    C) ALBERT CAMUS

HAVE YOU EVER CHANGED YOUR MIND IN THE MIDDLE OF
    AN ARGUMENT
    COURSE OF EDUCATION
    LONG-HAUL FLIGHT   OR
    RELATIONSHIP

DO YOU EVER FIND THE KINDNESS OF STRANGERS
    OVERWHELMING

DO EVERYDAY OBJECTS EVER APPEAR TO BE SUDDENLY
    OF UNUSUAL SIZE AND SHAPE

DO YOU EVER FEEL THE NEED TO SPEND SEVERAL DAYS
    STARING BLANKLY AT THE WALL AND MOANING

EACH OF THESE DAYS WILL BE CHARGED AT AN
    EXPONENTIAL RATE

HAVE YOU EVER BEEN BROUGHT TO TEARS BY
    THE BEAUTY
OF A PIECE OF ART OR NATURAL LANDSCAPE

WERE YOU ABLE TO CONTROL THESE FEELINGS   OR
DID YOU BUCKLE UNDER THE RUSH OF IT ALL

WOULD YOU LIKE TO PROCEED

ARE YOU SURE

Crossed Wires II: Council Tax

I swipe upward on the cracked Android
and a voice asks if I am aware
that I am three months in arrears
on my Council Tax payments.

I tell the voice that only this afternoon
I saw ten thousand starlings tear a hole right through the sky
and from that hole a cinnamon wind came blowing
spreading heather husks like confetti onto the road.

It's as the voice is asking for my account number
that I begin to talk about your eyes
I say, *I don't know when I first noticed it exactly*
but for some time now the blue of his eyes
has begun to take on a new depth,
    as if they've turned to glass.

The voice declares that there might be ways
to help me with the payments
at which point I say, *I think it might've happened*
while we were watching Master Chef.

The voice insists on the need to ask some security questions
and I exclaim, *exactly! If only you could be sure*
of the risk beforehand, it might not feel so much
like back-flipping drunk into a black lake.

...

I am unsure that the voice has grasped my point
but I was once informed that 93% of communication is non-verbal
so I make some expressive gestures at the handset
trying to convey the movement of the breeze
lifting the parched buds of heather from their stalks
the darkened hue of the blue of your eyes.

When I return my ear to the speaker
the voice has been replaced by a synthetic piano sound
and for a moment it seems as though
we're getting closer to an understanding.

But then the voice is back, saying
please bear with me while I transfer you to my colleague
and I am spinning out into the street
saying   *transfer away   I don't belong here anyway.*

Thunder and Sunshine

There's a thickness in my head and I'm sure it's not my brain / there's a thick, grey matter in my head and it's not my brain / if anything it's oozing its way between the capillaries of my brain and blocking off all normal communication between the nerve endings / it's turning all thought into a grey senseless throbbing / perhaps it's because I've been thinking too much / I've been thinking a lot recently / perhaps it's because I've been drinking too much / I've been drinking a lot recently / perhaps it might be a good idea if I lie down on the grass for a while / I remember as a child I used to wonder why the grass around ancient monuments was always softer and springier and greener and finer than the grass anywhere else / I've been remembering a lot recently / I've been remembering and forgetting and thinking a lot / the only time I haven't been thinking is right before I open my mouth / I've been thinking about what you said / I've been thinking about what you didn't say / I've been thinking that sometimes it's enough just to be surrounded by human voices / and sometimes it's not enough even when they're telling you they love you / have you ever looked out of the window and seen a face staring back at you / have you ever looked into the mirror and seen a clear view stretching out to sea / I've been thinking about sunstroke and Munich and Bovril and hair loss   and shyness and diamonds and siblings and skin   and carrots and rabbits and transplants and implants   and polygamy and Miles Davis and the House of Lords and the rain   and the unbearable sadness   of the fact that   some things are   and some things aren't.

...

And whilst I've been thinking and remembering and lying on the grass / I've become aware of a rumble in the distance and it's not the throbbing of my brain / there's a rumble and I'm sure it's not the throbbing of my brain / and as I'm hearing it I'm sure a single raindrop taps me surreptitiously on the shoulder / but when I look around I'm greeted by the mocking mirthless face of a grinning yellow sun / and the effort of looking upwards presses the poisonous grey matter against the back of my eyeballs / and it hurts and it hurts and it hurts / and the sky is thick like the thickness in my head   and I think   if we're going to have a monsoon   will we become like India   will we no longer have irony or queuing or porridge or whist   but colour and chaos and karma and cows   and would it be better that way   or would it be better if everything just stopped   for a while   and would it be better if I stood up for while   and would it be better if you could stop   thinking   just for a while?

If You Know What I Mean

If you're the sort
who nightmares every morning

if you're the sort
who rabbits in the headlights

if you're the sort
who thunders home, ungiving
won't admit, not until

the cold light
of a bedside candle
in an old wine bottle
on a plastic table
in a caravan
on a coastline
in the weeping arms
of a giant.

If you're the sort
who spaghetti-junctions to the bar again
gin-slings yet another unspent evening

cries

because forgetting what it felt like not to grip the brakes
    forgetting what it felt like
        to close your eyes and only darkness
            close your eyes and only darkness

                                                  ...

forgetting what it felt like
    to o p e n your eyes and   only   world.

If you're the sort
who awkwards in the hairdresser's

because how can you be so trimmings of truth
    and how can you be so sweepings on the floor
        and how can you be so classless and masked.

If jealous eyes are waiting for you
at midnight in the hallway

if wife at home
is half-way down the bottle
is too tired to be drunk
is too tired to be drunk by you
the way you used to drink her
half-way down her bottle.

If vein in your temple
has been throbbing
for longer than memory

if you're restless
if you're scared
if you know what I mean

if you know what I mean.

From *The Unsung*

The following poems originally appeared in a stage show incorporating music from a live band, which celebrated forgotten heroes who lost their lives to music.

Air on a Heart-String

For Sandor Feher (1974 – 2012),
violinist, who after playing in the string quartet on the Costa
Concordia cruise ship, died when the ship started to sink after
returning to his cabin to fetch his violin.

If you'd known it were the calm before the storm
you might've noticed something uncanny or unreal
in the way the light reflected back and forth
a thousand times between champagne flute and chandelier.

You might've seen in the fine, red, wine-red
wine-sloshed posh-clothed soft furnishings
messages of warning painted in blood
and you might've known that the to and fro
and to and fro and to and fro
was not the gentle lilting of a lolling ship at sea
but its lulling you into a false sense of security.

But there were no storm-clouds
no warnings or forecasts or blood-red skies
no distant rumblings or omens from on-high
nothing sinister in the *ching!*
of glass-on-crystal glass
or ring of laugh on cackling laugh
or string of bow on violin, and so
you only felt the calm.

Perhaps if you had known that you were sounding your last notes
you might've played a different tune to keep their hopes afloat
something poignant   something perfect   something truly virtuoso
plucked upon a heart-string, *pizzicato lacrimoso*
oh-so soulful-sweetly you'd have spilled into their ears
the slow-fast   fast-slow   last-slow-dance romance flow of your bow
like salt-water weeping into pores, chords falling
like waves crescendo-crashing under skin
the last tune you would hear before you
diminuendoed deep back down within
where your heart-beat double-stopped, and you
were rhapsodied in blue
raptured in a shroud of sound.

The Eagles of Death

For the 89 victims (d.2015)
of the terrorist attack on the Bataclan concert hall, Paris, during a concert by The Eagles of Death Metal.

Funny how you always remember where you were
on days the world goes wrong

like when the twin towers fell
I was walking home from school
and eating a Calippo.

On days like those everything seems to happen
in ultra-high definition – I can remember vividly
the sweetness freezing on my tongue
the syrup dripping thickly down my fingers.

This time, I was pulling pints
hearing the news by way of gossip flung across the bar.

I checked my phone, where newspaper apps
had packaged the story into screen-shaped one-liners
the numbers all mixed up but always rising.

The word *Terror* was being splashed around like ready cash
but somehow it had lost all meaning
and the letters seem to crawl like ants
out from the display and over my hands.

I moved out from the bar and into the garden
where I sat watching the river
trying to picture the scene
before the ants nest was disturbed.

***

A concert hall, waiting
all decked out in red velvet and polished brass
floors swept and chewing gum removed
from underneath the seats.

The silence is broken by thick slices of electric guitar
levels being checked though great black stacks lining the walls.

Backstage, vocal cords are warmed and fingers limbered up
jokes are cracked like eggs on the dressing room floor.

In his home in the eleventh arrondissement
Matthieu Giroud, 38, plays a few bars of his own on bass
causing his three-year old son to wake
and its mother to warn him, half-serious
that he'd better get going before he's late.

As he pulls the front door shut
he does not see the eagles circling overhead.

In other parts of town carpenters, surfers and lawyers
change into blue jeans
line their stomachs with chips and mayonnaise
telephone friends
open bottles of Pinot Noir.

...

Graphic designers pack up their pencils
and try to leave work on time.

A grandmother, mother and son
bundle each other in Spanish onto the bus.

An eagle surveys the scene from its perch atop the bus stop.

The city is humming, minding its own frantic business
ant-like trails are traced from all corners
towards the concert hall.

But on the rooftops
the eagles are flexing their gnarled claws
and clicking their hooked beaks
getting ready to strike.

Lola Ouzounian, 17, Franco-Armenian
is choosing between two T-shirts
laid out side by side on her bed.

She has the radio on loud
so she does not hear the eagles calling out into the night.

Lola was born on the bridge between East and West
in a cradle of division
but there were eagles nesting under the bridge
and when she went West they never forgave her.

Lola is excited for her first gig, a night out with Dad.
At exactly her age, for me it was my elder brother
and The Manic Street Preachers at Leeds Metropolitan.

The same year I marched through London with a placard that read
NOT IN MY NAME
I can remember painting on the letters myself
in thick red ink outlined in black.

On the coach trip down my brother told me
some quotes by Einstein and Aldous Huxley
and I wrote them on the covers of my schoolbooks
but I never looked up at the sky.

***

And now the eagles are circling again.

They are hiding amongst the gargoyles of Notre Dame
they are swooping down the Seine
they are in congress on the chimney stacks.

And the ants are scribbling through the streets
and the river is flowing past the pub
and the syrup is dripping through my fingers
and letters spell names in thick red ink
and Lola is choosing the wrong T-shirt
and the eagles dive out from under the bridge
and my brother is saying a thousand new words
and the newspapers fight over who thought it first.

***

Funny how you always remember where you were
on days the world goes wrong.

...

That day I shivered in the empty beer garden
watching the street lights shimmer on the surface of the
Sheaf.

Only this time I remembered to look up at the sky

and I saw black shadows circling
and I heard the eagles crying out for blood.

The Fiery Angel

For Lina Prokofiev (1897 – 1989),
wife of composer Sergei Prokofiev, who was arrested by the
Russian secret police in 1948 and committed to a concentration
camp for eight years. During this time, she wrote to Prokofiev
asking him to help her get out, but he refused, preferring to stay
with his mistress. In his letters he likened Lina to an 'infected
tooth', but she remained faithful, and continued to champion his
music and their love until her death.

I never want to love like Lina Prokofiev;
not like Juliet, Anna Karenina, Sylvia Plath
Cathy Earnshaw or Madame Butterfly.

I never want to feel the way that first chord feels
discord twisting your guts up around your spine
stringing you up high and dry
I never want to die inside for someone else's life
I never want to die in your arms   in your grip
under a spell   under a train   in vain
by my own hand or yours   by my own sick heart
I'd rather die   alone.

I never want to miss you more
than I miss the self I wrote out of my own love letters

I will not lie back on the sand
and let the music wash over me

I want to be the music.

...

Because there is nothing beautiful about standing in the shadow
of anyone who picks you up and rams you into their world
without a care for where you came from
only to rip you out again like an infected tooth
there is nothing beautiful about three and a half months
    without sleep
there is nothing beautiful about torture.

And so I will not let you be the one to sing me to sleep
I will not let you sing me to delirious, half-awake half-sleep
I do not want your lullaby
I want to be the music.

And when the world asks if your love
was as sublime as the music that it spawned
if the love that fired the fiery angel
was as hot   and raw   and fraught
as the taut strings of the violins
that sting at the heartstrings of any soul that hears them
I will not bow my head and say
we worked together for the music.

And yes, I'd rather not have loved at all
than have loved and lost
if losing means walking ten feet behind your husband
honouring and obeying or baying at the moon
crying for a pain you've been made slave to.

I never want to love like Lina Prokofiev;
not like Juliet, Anna Karenina, Sylvia Plath
Cathy Earnshaw or Madame Butterfly.

I will not lie back on the sand
and let the music wash over me

I want to be the music.

The Unsung

For musicians in Mali (2012-2013)
resisting a militant extremist ban on live music.

If I could sing
I'd sing a song for all the folks
who've struggled to be heard.

For musicians in exile
youth orchestra conductors
drunk uncles and little sisters.

For Maya Angelou and Gil Scot Heron
for Pussy Riot and The Plastic People of the Universe
for Scott Johnson and Lina Prokofiev.

If I could sing
I'd sing for Mali
whose mouth was once covered by a dead man's hand
for its ghost towns gathering dust
streets and schoolyards hushed
for the microphones and amplifiers
squealing in toxic bonfires
kora strings pinged from their pegs
by flickering tongues of flame
for the doors smashed in by AK-47 butts
hanging limply from their frames.

If I could sing
I'd sing in Karaoke booths
in church
in the shower

I'd stand under your window
and serenade you with songs about your hair

I'd sail into your harbour
singing shanties about sea monsters and storms.

I'd sing a song for Mali
for Toumani Diabaté
Amkoullel and Rokia Traoré
for those who did not stop singing
lungs full and faces brave
for the memory of Ali Farka Touré
still spinning in his grave
for the dismembered head of Edwin Dyer
caught in the wrong place.

If I could sing
I'd probably be singing right now instead of talking
If I could sing
I'd write a concept album about dead poets

If I could sing
I'd sing for Mali
for Scirocco, the maddening wind
that curdles chaos in its belly
for the dry heat of the desert
for blistered feet and dust-choked lungs.

If I could sing
I'd sing for sweaty gigs in run down pubs
for spending the whole night in the smoking area
for pissing off the neighbours
for campfires and football matches

for punch-drunk post-punks
for sycophantic new romantics
for mods and rockers and fashion shockers
for all night raves and songs of praise
and northern soul and rock and roll
and golden oldies oversold
in bargain bins in record shops
and rich kids miming on *Top of the Pops*.

If I could sing
I'd sing for Mali
where music is the crude oil
locked inside the very bedrock.

If I could sing
I'd go into the desert and cry out into the night
and my voice would tremble down through the granite
and be carried away on the mad dry wind
and resound in every corner of the mad old world
and never stop

and never ever stop.

Exit Music

For Scott Johnson (1979 – 2012),
drum technician, who died when the stage collapsed on
top of him when setting up for Radiohead in Canada.

Check.
Check.

- A technician sits behind a drum kit -

check one *tap*
check one *tap*

- on an empty stage three hours before the show -

check one two *tap tap*
check one two *tap tap*

- sticks in hand he tests each component in turn -

check the kick drum *thud*
check the toms *ta ta tap*
check the hi-hat *t-t-ch t-t-ch!*
check the tiny little screws
that snap the snare on tighter than tight
check the pedal mechanisms
check the height of the stands
check the cymbals *crasssshhhhh*
check *everything is in its right place* .

...

- The technician looks around swiftly -

check that no-one's looking

- and starts to play -

check yourself out
five minutes of fame
five imaginary thousand
screaming out your name
drum-roll   solo   *crash bang wollop*
sing a song   tell a joke   **baddum tch!**

- then stops. –

Check yourself
back to work
setting stage
tuning up
paving later's way.

- As he leaves the kit and starts to lug equipment about thoughts flit half-consciously through his mind -

check you locked the back door
before you left the house
check you took the bins out
make sure you defrosted the chicken
or you'll be eating late again tonight

- but as his dilly-dally daydreams drift off deeper he doesn't notice that the plywood cave around him is beginning to creak uneasily -

check you were on your best behaviour
when the in-laws came to stay
make sure you didn't say anything risqué
check you fit the mould
check you know you're place
check you've always got a smile on your face

- and suddenly the stage supports
begin to brace, brace, bend, buckle, break!
and before he knows it, they're upon him -

check you made your mother and father proud
check you left your grandchildren something to pass down
check you told your loved ones they were loved once
because this could be your last chance
this could be your final cadence

check you told your loved ones they were loved once
because it may just be that today's the day
your world will come cymbal-crashing-thrashing down on you
like fraying threads the fibres of your life may splinter and unwind
and sounded out by booming dooming drums
you, who an ear-split-second before
was so alive and breathing heaving deep
you, who clattered in and out of other people's lives
may stop   still   stock-still

may rest in pieces of your former self.

...

- And after the collapse, he lies there
still and quiet. But listen closely
and a single trace rings out
beyond his flesh and blood.
Listen closely, and you can still hear
the remnants of a tune - his exit music
spinning, spinning in his still warm ear
like spinning plates beginning to lose momentum
slowing now, circling flatter until they hit the floor
then   silence.   -

So check you're ready to check out
make sure you leave history a legacy to shout about
check you didn't waste all your time
double-checking shit that didn't matter
check you let your skeletons out of their cupboards
and make sure they crumbled every inch to dust

check you've made peace with your demons
and been good to your fellow man
say your prayers at night and don't forget to say *Amen.*

Check you told your loved ones they were loved once
because this could be your last chance
this could be your final cadence

check you told your loved ones they were loved once
because the show just might be over
and we're not sound-checking anymore.

A Beautiful Way to be Crazy

In the UK at the time of publication, 70% of music acts are all-male.

The following poems originally appeared in a stage show incorporating music from a live band, about female experiences in the music industry.

The show was researched through interviews with almost 50 female and non-binary practitioners across the music industry. Quotes from these interviews are included alongside the poems (initials do not correspond to any real names).

Prelude

R: There's some kind of power in holding a guitar, or being behind a drum kit, and so many girls will never know what that feels like.
S: We're starting to understand that history so far has been very much made up by white men. That's great, we've achieved a lot with that, but what could we achieve if we stopped seeing the boundaries as so fixed, and started to question things more..?

It was easy for me.

I was taught to read and write
and I learned well, got the best grades.
My home was full of music
and I was shown love
boundless as grief.

I got here easy enough
crawled out of adolescence
into some vague, undefined need to express myself.
Like anyone, people gave me shit along the way
but people were kind too
and it didn't seem so far to walk up here
and say a few words.

Except it did.

It was easy for me
but still I had to stop hating myself long enough
not to tear up every word I wrote
had to beat back the stinging rash
that spread under my skin like wildfire
infecting every fibre
with the *hisssss* that *I'll never be good enough.*

I had to learn somehow to live with this body
(or at best inside it, but never really *be* it)
despite it being at once oversized and not enough
despite it veering wildly out of tune with itself like a
        w a r p e d record
despite the stench of rotting meat.

I had to swallow the lump in my throat
that only wants to spit out saltwater
like a storm-whipped ocean spluttering onto shore
asking *why the hell is everyone looking at me.*

I had to be heckled in the street so many times
I started to keep stones in my pockets
which I never threw
but used to take comfort from the fact they were there
as if in some perverse way I got to know how it feels
to have a pair of bollocks.

I had to bear the touch of unwanted hands
to be called every name under the shame-faced sun
to be told to cover up because the sight of my flesh
reminds him of the whore I am.

                                                     ...

It was easy enough, for me, to get here
but still there were times it felt like scaling an impenetrable
    castle wall
the tips of my fingers gripping hard stone
clawing my way between thorns and wading through swamps
trying not to get caught in the crossfire
trying to keep my eyes pointing up
thinking   *God*   *I just hope when I get there*
I can remember what it was   *that I wanted to say.*

                                                         ...

It's Alright, Dad (I'm Only Disappearing)

N: I feel like what stopped me doing music as a teenager was definitely confidence.
L: When I was younger I had much lower confidence than I have now and a lot of that was down to being in bands that were all boys.

My bedroom wall is a shrine
to who I think I want to be
topless boys wield guitars
that wail a song I cannot sing along to
and there's no space left
between the noise for thinking.

I'd like to take a rubber to myself
and sketch my outline anew
but I am being inked in
the numbers you paint me by do not add up
I never knew that growing
could feel so much like shrinking.

The spiral in the sand becomes a shell
the shell becomes ammonite etched in stone
the stone skims o h - s o - briefly on the surface
but it's alright Dad, I'm only sinking.

On the stereo in the corner
Bob Dylan skips on his jog wheel
freewheeling seems so easy to him
but how was he so sure his fight was worth fighting.

...

I am nothing but echo, soft shell crab
putty in your hands
be gentle when you mould me
watch closely where you guide me

there's an aeon to pass 'til my driving test
and of driving I must learn not only how
but also in which direction
when you ask me why I mask my face in paint
I can only answer
it's alright Mum, I'm only hiding.

My hair is purple and my clothes are black
my eyelids carefully lined to match
but there are times I lift my folding pocket mirror
and nobody looks back

everybody's staring at me
but I can't catch a single eye
*everybody's talking at me
but I don't hear a word.*

I place my palm on the photograph of Chopin's hands
inside the cover of my piano book
my fingertips reach his knuckles
and I ask him how I'll ever fill the space between us
but my ears are blocked again with noise
a nocturne drowning in a drone of jeering.

The moon is full and I am were-wolfing
Frankensteining   monster turning into
I am square peg boring into round wound
I am clinging onto   Peter Panning
running home   to nowhere

my limbs are driftwood tossed to shore
my bones are rotten at the core
the playing fields are wide and bleak
I do not have a team I wander lonely
I am shadowless   oblique

but it's alright Dad
it's alright
I'm only   disappearing.

This Stage Ain't Big Enough for the Both of Us

For Faustina Bordoni and Francesca Cuzzoni, aka 'Handel's divas'

A: There are some women who I've found it difficult to work with because there is a real competitive element...we're made to feel that we have to prove ourselves, and that includes trampling each other down.

A mirror hangs on the dressing room wall
we stand before it   side   by   side
every stroke of the powder brush loaded with expectation
hope coiled in the ringlets we curl between our fingers.

A mirror hangs on the dressing room wall
we stand before it in supposed solidarity
but there's something bubbling beneath the surface
friction prickling like static under our skin.

Neither of us knows what to say
so we bounce passive-aggressive platitudes off the glass
nice hair / I love what you haven't done with it /
I've never been brave enough for such a casual look.

A mirror hangs on the dressing room wall
and a thousand pairs of eyes
shine through it
fixed on our faces that crease and squirm

with every insecurity ever borne
every word that ever made us feel small
rebounding back
                between us infinitely.

Neither of us knows what to say
so we swallow our readiness to fail
and let the resentment slowly build
it's all we can do to smile

and wish each other luck
but before long this lump in the throat
is going to burst
and erupt like lava from our lips

we've bottled it up 'til we're ready to pop
like a bloated cork at the devil's wedding reception
this tension is too taut to bear
too heavy to hold, too hot to handle.

A mirror hangs on the dressing room wall
and we begin to warm our vocal chords
two voices rising higher and higher
until we're fighting to be heard

the gloves are off / we've had enough
abandon the facts / stab in the back
I'll rip her to shreds / I wish she were dead
she's full of shit / the cheek of it
she's stolen everything she's got from me
she's tried to build the best version
of herself upon my shoulders
but the worst is on my chest

she is the echo chamber screaming back
we are a nightmare hall of mirrors
in case of emergency break glass
can't stand it / can't hack it /
can't handle it anymore.

A mirror hangs on the dressing room wall
and we count slowly to four
before we rise and make our way across the floor
a quick glace in the mirror

and we're ready to face our fears
the curtain lifts   and we disappear.

Human Being (a pop song)

"Pulling on her tracks
hit her from the back
and now she's screaming out 'no más'" – Post Malone
(2017), Rockstar. (UK Top 40 Chart).

M: You are not supposed to feel any other way than ashamed. You are
never supposed to feel comfortable in your body, in yourself, ever.
G: It's basically my responsibility in the band to be the hot one, to be
the one that everyone looks at
L: I would describe most chart music as completely vapid.

Girl when I first saw you
you really had me gawpin'
never seen a woman move
that way across the floor

you said *what the fuck*
are you staring at
and smacked me in the jaw
and from that moment I was sure

that I wanted to possess you
caress you, get under your dress
you hit me harder this time but I wasn't giving up
girl you look so fine when you say you've had enough.

On our first date we went out on a Groupon voucher
2-4-1 dunno what I'd do without ya
but I couldn't believe it at the end of the meal
when you paid half the bill, I said *girl are you for real.*

As we walked away from Nandos
I was feeling anxious
wondering if my pride could survive
not being the man though

you took me by the hand
said *babe you gotta understand
there's no shame in the equal division of power
between woman and man, no.*

> *Girl when I close my eyes I see
> inside your body there's a human being
> got thoughts in your head you deserve respect
> you're a human being you're not an object.*

On our second date you took me to see
The Vagina Monologues - it's not a ping-pong show
it a piece of seminal feminist theatre
I went just because I wanted to be near ya

but I learned a lot about two female organs
the vagina and the brain and I know it sounds insane
but I'm starting to believe these babes
they've really got something to say.

On the way home we stopped
at a bar we were passing
we raised a little glass
we got a little smashed

then I took you back
and we listened to Ed Sheeran records
until you screamed out
>
> *no más!*

> *Girl when I close my eyes I see*
> *inside your body there's a human being*
> *got thoughts in your head you deserve respect*
> *you're a human being you're not an object.*

You said we couldn't have a third date until
I'd read *The Second Sex* by Simone de Beauvoir
when I saw it was 800 pages long
I though our relationship was over

I was even more dismayed to find
there's barely any sex inside
but six months later I'd read it cover to cover
and I'd learnt a thing or two about sisters and mothers.

Girl this equality vibe got me winding
wish I could grind your mind
it's tiring rhyming every line
but you get the gist so I'll say goodbye.

> *Girl when I close my eyes I see*
> *inside your body there's a human being*
> *got thoughts in your head you deserve respect*
> *you're a human being you're not an object.*

Little Green
For Joni Mitchell

B: I haven't been in the profession because I chose to put my kids first. I have loads of female colleagues that didn't do that and I admire and respect them, but I wanted to be at home...and yes, I felt like I'd never be able to go back into performing again.

Lullabies are not really my thing / I find it kind of hard to look small children in the eyes / you may be all innocence and hope now/ but sooner or later you're gonna find out about the world you've been born into / and for that I can only apologise / I'm not really sure where to start / so I guess I'll start with Joni Mitchell / I've always found her voice to ring kind of true / so Joni had a little girl like you / but she had to give her up / *I'm sure she did love her but it was more complicated than that* / you see she wrote this song, 'Little Green' / *no don't cry, I'm trying to explain* / there's a thing called *organized religion* which makes some people act very unfairly sometimes / and there's a thing called money which you sort of need if you / *no please don't cry*

> *Lullabies don't come naturally to me*
> *but if I were going to sing you one*
> *I'd sing you Joni Mitchell's Little Green.*

Lullabies, they're supposed to be calming aren't they / so perhaps I should tell you that there's nothing you need to worry about right now / just look at the little felt stars dangling above your cot / try to focus on the beauty of the moment / because much sooner than you think you're gonna wake up one day to find your body is decaying / and your mind is haunted by regrets / and you're having to make some serious redacts to your bucket list / *no, shhhh, forget that* / I know that somewhere out there there's a parallel universe / and parallel me is kneeling by your bedside / reading you the poems of Shakespeare's sister / her verses are spiralling elegantly from my mouth / flitting around the cradle like moths to a candle / and in that cradle there's a little parallel you / who will grow up to have a room of her own / and her destiny will not be coded into the figure her father's bank account / *it's a place where people put money so that people with more money can use it to make more money from the people with less money / in and of itself it doesn't really do anything but you can use it to make stuff happen / sometimes it's invisible and sometimes it's made of paper / the best type is called dollars and it's green, like the song -*

> Lullabies don't come naturally to me
> but if I were going to sing you one
> I'd sing you Joni Mitchell's Little Green.

Ok, *shhh now*, it's getting late / all I was trying to say was Joni had a lot of unseen pressure on her from this thing called *society* / *you know, like the idea that every woman is either a mother, a potential mother or a failed mother* / I'd just like you to know that you don't have to grow up to be any of those / *no there's nothing wrong with it it's just that people don't always see men like that* / and if the only purpose of humans is to make more humans then what exactly is the purpose of making more humans / we've already spread across the entire planet like a plague wiping out tigers and rainforests and dolphins and ice flows with every bit of plastic ever made piling up in our wake torturing and enslaving and raping each other only stopping to send hateful tweets to minor celebrities about the cellulite in their thighs greedy fingers poised on big red buttons like some grotesque game of nuclear chicken / sometimes I just feel like more humans is not necessarily the best idea / *no of course I'm glad you were born / I'm sorry if this isn't helping you sleep / I told you I was never any good at lullabies* -

> *Lullabies don't come naturally to me*
> *but if I were going to sing you one*
> *I'd sing you Joni Mitchell's Little Green.*

We Don't Need Another Hero
IM Ike Turner

H: So you're the first to war and the last in the life boat, how do you feel?
O: If one of the guys isn't doing what's seen to be masculine there's a concern of being picked on or victimized.
F: I really think it affects guys too, and a lot of guys I work with really hate that whole macho culture.

Dear Ike,

You were a real scumbag
and I'm sorry for that.

I'm sorry you had to swallow the fear
swimming in your father's eyes

that you had to be the shock absorber
for your stepdad's pain.

I'm sorry you almost buckled
under your mother's knuckles

that instead of tears there was only vodka
instead of lullabies, only war cries
and power games in place of first-kiss butterflies.

...

I'm sorry you manned up
that you took all that
chicken-shit lily-livered limp-wristed
yellow-bellied namby-pamby
pansy pussy wuss wimp sissy
faggot fairy shit
and made a grenade in your chest from it.

I'm sorry nobody ever told you
that to be vulnerable is not to be weak
that to be weak is not shameful
that there's no shame in being unsure
that nobody is sure of anything.

I was wrong to think we girls
had the monopoly on shame

I was wrong to believe you had it all sussed
just because you said you did

I just hope I'm not wrong in expecting better.

I'm sorry that if you had been
that misty-eyed stranger at the bar

whispering into his whisky for me
to listen just for a minute
I'd definitely have turned away.

I'm sorry we never went blackberry picking
or laughed each other's worries away
on cycle rides down leafy lanes.

I'm sorry the bass couldn't ground you
that the rhythm never rocked you right

that you had to die alone
with a clean white lance
driven through your heart

like a real man.

The Canary in the Coal Mine

"The artist is the canary in the coal mine" – Joni Mitchell

H: Music is my community, my saviour, and my friend, but it's also so double edged - you can so easily slip into the dark side of egomania, drug addiction, alcoholism. There is that driving force of the 'making it myth' - when I get there everything will be alright - or you might kill yourself because it's really not alright. There's an expectation that it'll solve all your problems but it just shines a light on them brighter.
E: I aim to find my self-esteem from within me, then if I do have a bad gig it doesn't crush me, because my self-worth isn't based on each success.

I had this dream I was a little yellow bird
and they sent me down the mine

my feathers were speckled with coal dust
but still I shone brightly as I went down
                                        down
and down there in the depths

I found a warren of beauty and shadows
darkness and light   doorways and passages
and figures moving   and a thousand songs being sung.

I dreamt I was a melody wisping from a magic flute
but my notes were all off-pitch
and anyhow no-one could hear me

I just hung in the air all out of key and breathless
like a murder ballad's ghost.

I dreamt that I was falling through the strings of a giant harp
I dreamt a familiar stranger came to invade my heart

I dreamt a man in a shiny blue suit made me sign my life away
I dreamt I was on stage naked and I had nothing to say.

And I woke in cold sweat
writhing, twitching
questions spinning round
                    and round the room

will I make the train   did I lock the door
will anyone come   have I got it all wrong
am I gaining weight   am I losing ground
am I still attractive to men
      am I really here at all
        who am I.

And then I was back in the coal mine
with fear brushing my wings
and love caught in my beak

and Janis Joplin was asking
What Good Can Drinking Do
but I couldn't reply
because I was drowning in an ocean of gin

and Billie Holiday was asking
Why Was I Born
but I couldn't reply
because I had turned into a violin.

...

And the headmaster was asking me
to explain myself

and the wedding guests were politely asking
and what do you do

and HMRC were asking me
to return the form below

and Amy Winehouse was asking
do I want another line

and my back was breaking
and my pockets were full of stones
and the water was rising
and my ears throbbed with the most distorted refrain
and my lungs were full of thick black smoke
and I was choking   choking   on myself.

And I woke in cold sweat
writhing, twitching
questions spinning round
                      and round the room

and again I became that twisted tune
and I floated softly away over the rooftops
echoed through the sleeping streets

leaving nothing behind but a streak of soot
across the crumpled sheets.

A Beautiful Way to be Crazy
IM Delia Derbyshire

A found poem comprised entirely of soundbites from interviews with female-identifying musicians.

How do you get in
        and do you even want to get in?

I listened very carefully / I practiced for hours and hours until a tiny thing would happen / it was like nothing else existed / I got lost for days / I couldn't block out the outside world / my life wouldn't let me / when I wasn't playing, I grieved.

It was like someone had turned the creative tap on / it was like the background hum had been switched off / it was my heart and soul / it was summat to do / it felt safe / I felt safe and happy / I didn't always feel safe.

I never in a million years thought I'd do music / I never thought I'd be doing this / I never thought I'd play an instrument on stage / my dad would have said *don't be so fucking stupid* / I didn't decide to be a singer / I didn't decide to be a woman / I didn't decide to be gay.

I wish I had been stronger / I wish I'd learned to take things apart / I would have liked to have made noise / I'm scared of pressing the wrong button / I'm scared of mirrors / I'm scared of everything / my worst fear was that someone would find out I had body hair.

                                                                  ...

I don't want to reveal who I am / I'm still finding out who I am / it's as much to find out what I'm not as what I am / it took a lot of strength to leave and become myself / I'm on a personal mission to know myself better / I've only just started to scratch the surface of thinking for myself / I'm giving myself more permission to be more myself every time.

I wear confidence like armour / I've learned to be confident / on the inside I'm cowering / you can start to get paranoid / I had to take myself off Facebook because it sent me mad.

We do it to ourselves / it's my own fault / I have a problem with being self-critical / I'm my own worst critic / I'm just fucking brilliant / I always believed I could do it.

My playing was different to his / I'm more of a bloke than half of them out there / we care about the detail / we care about the bigger picture / it's more holistic / it's more responsive / *how would the music sound if it were equal* / there might be another world out there I didn't know about / we're heading in the right direction / we've come so far / we're so far away / people are reading the *Daily Mail* unashamedly.

Music is in me all the time / I feel lucky / it helps me get my feelings back / it's therapy / it's my diary / it's my saviour / but does it mean anything / does anyone care / in the end you don't really have a choice / it feels like once you start you can't get away from it –

we have to make stuff
        or we'll go crazy.

Champagne, Cocaine & Sausages

"I want champagne, cocaine and sausages" – Nina Simone.

L: *You can't be what you can't see, so if you see somebody on stage who looks like you, you can see yourself in that position.*

I am Nina Simone's anger
I am Etta James's veins
I am Ani DiFranco's middle finger
I am your little sister's bedroom door.

I am the ripple in the pond
I am the rip in your jeans
I am wild and unwashed and broken
I am not taking it lying down.

I am shit at lots of things
I am difficult
I am wrong
I am tied in knots   I'm free
I am simply trying to be me
I am frightened
I am flawed
but I am here
and I'm not going anywhere.

I am Kate Bush's treble
I am Jacqueline du Pres' tremble
I am Polly Harvey's pedals
I am Kathleen Hanna's rebel.

...

I am Clara Schuman's manuscript
I am Stevie Nicks's sleeves
I am Alanis Morisette's misunderstanding of irony
I am Bjork's clenched fist.

I'm just a girl
I wear my hair in curls
I wear my dungarees
down to my sexy knees
I am sugar and spice and all things
deep and lost and painful and real
I am fighting to be heard
and not only seen
I am a woman, phenomenally.

I am Tori Amos's cornflakes
I am Sinead O'Connor's skull
I am Taylor Swift's reputation
I am Madonna's youth.

I want champagne, cocaine and sausages
I want it all and I want it now
I want what I cannot have
I am hungry
I am greedy
I will bite off more than I can
vomit back into the void
it's a new dawn
it's a new day
it's a new life
and I'm feeling ready for it.

...

I am the reason the caged bird sings
I am the thorn in the side of the boy
I am the fat lady telling you it's over
I am spinning
I am floating
I am so close to the edge
I am busting at the seams
I am everything you ever hoped you'd be

so take a piece, just try it
there's too much here
for you to even make a dent in me.

NOTES:
Many of the poems in this book contain references to songs or individual quotes, the origins of which are listed here.

P21. *'Strong and Stable.'* Theresa May, 2017

P22. *'I'm into champagne.'* After Rupert Holmes (1979), *Escape (The Piña Colada Song)*. On *Partners in Crime*.

P35. *'Get loaded. Have a good time. Be free.'* Primal Scream (1991), *Loaded*. On *Screamadelica*.

P37. *'Hackenthorpe'* Pulp (1992), *Sheffield Sex City*. On *Babies (B-Side)*.

P37. *'...so please can I ask ...'* Pulp, (1998), *I'm a Man*. On *This is Hardcore*.

P49. *'rhapsodied in blue'* George Gershwin (1924), *Rhapsody in Blue*.

P55. *'The Fiery Angel.'* Sergei Prokofiev (1923), *The Fiery Angel*.

P61. *'Exit Music'* Radiohead (1997), *Exit Music (for a Film)*. On *OK Computer*.

P61. *'everything is in its right place'* Radiohead (2000), *Everything in its Right Place*. On *Kid A*.

P64. *'like spinning plates'* Radiohead (2001), *Like Spinning Plates*. On *Amnesiac*

P69. *'It's Alright, Dad...'* After Bob Dylan (1965), *It's Alright, Ma (I'm Only Bleeding)*. On *Bringing it all Back Home*.

P70. *'Everybody's talking at me...'* Harry Nilsson (1968), *Everybody's Talking at Me*. On *Aerial Ballet*.

P72. *'This town ain't...'* After Sparks (1974), *This Town Ain't Big Enough for the Both of Us*. On *Kimono My House*.

P78. *'Little Green'* Joni Mitchell (1971), *Little Green*. On *Blue*.

P79. *'Shakespeare's sister.'* Virginia Woolf (1929), *A Room of One's Own*.

P79. *'room of her own'* Virginia Woolf (1929), *A Room of One's Own*.

P81. *'We Don't Need...'* Tina Turner (1985), *We Don't Need Another Hero*.

P85. *'What Good Can Drinking Do'* Janis Joplin (1975), *What Good can Drinkin' Do*. On *Janis*.

P85. *'Why Was I Born'* Jerome Kern and Oscar Hammerstein II (1929), *Why Was I Born*, recorded by Billie Holiday in 1937.

P90. 'I am a woman...' Maya Angelou (1995), *Phenomenal Woman*.

P90. 'It's a new dawn...' Nina Simone (1965), *Feeling Good*. On *I Put a Spell on You*.

P91 'I'm the reason...' After Maya Angelou (1969), *I Know Why the Caged Bird Sings*.

P91. .The thorn in the side...' After The Smiths (1985), *The Boy with the Thorn in his Side*.

A huge thank you to:

Brian Bestall, Ruth Nicholson and Tim Knowles (The Unsung) for the music, for being my team, and for helping me to grow as an artist.

Every female-identifying music practitioner that let me interview them and write about them for *A Beautiful Way to be Crazy*.

Charlotte Ansell, Joe Kriss, Rose Condo, Freddie Carver and Ciarán Hodgers for your comments on early drafts of this book, and Stuart Bartholomew for editorial support.

Arts Council England for helping to fund the research and development of both *The Unsung* and *A Beautiful Way to be Crazy*.

The editors of *Iota, Now Then* and *Wordlife 10*, where some of these poems first appeared.

My family and friends for believing in me, Joe Kriss and Gav Roberts for your support from the very beginning, Emily Compton for your positivity and perspective, and Chris Lockyer for your patience, understanding and love.

ABOUT VERVE POETRY PRESS

Verve Poetry Festival is a new press focussing initially on meeting a local need in Birmingham - a need for the vibrant poetry scene here in Brum to find a way to present itself to the poetry world via publication. Co-founded by Stuart Bartholomew and Amerah Saleh, it is publishing poets from all corners of the city - poets that represent the city's varied and energetic qualities and will communicate its many poetic stories.

Added to this is a colourful pamphlet series featuring poets who have previously performed at our sister festival - and a poetry show series which captures the magic of longer poetry performance pieces by poets such as Polarbear, Matt Abbott and now Genevieve Carver.

Like the festival, we strive to think about poetry in inclusive ways and embrace the multiplicity of approaches towards this glorious art.

www.vervepoetrypress.com
@VervePoetryPres
mail@vervepoetrypress.com